D1519491

How to Find Calm in Five Minutes a Day

JOANNE MALLON

circus

HOW TO FIND CALM IN FIVE MINUTES A DAY

An Hachette UK Company
www.hachette.co.uk

Circus Books, an imprint of Summersdale Publishers Ltd
Part of Octopus Publishing Group Limited
Carmelite House
50 Victoria Embankment
LONDON
EC4Y 0DZ
UK

www.summersdale.com

Printed and bound in China

ISBN: 978-1-83799-219-5

Substantial discounts on bulk quantities of Summersdale books are available to corporations, professional associations and other organizations. For details contact general enquiries by telephone: +44 (0) 1243 771107 or email: enquiries@summersdale.com

10 9 8 7 6 5 4 3 2

Contents

Introduction

Today's world is anything but calm. Stress bombards us every day, and if we don't pause for peace, we risk becoming overwhelmed.

These pages contain suggestions, ideas and inspiration to help you connect to calm. They will guide you through a day in your life, with suggestions as to where you might find pockets of quiet and tranquillity.

If there's a time of day when you feel particularly overloaded, read through the appropriate section for ideas about how to rise above the storm and recentre yourself. Pick a tip that resonates with you and try it out for a few days.

You can complete these tips in under 5 minutes, and many in much less time than that. The aim is not to overload your life but to support you as you carry your burdens. Pausing regularly for a little calm and peace will help smooth out the chaos of everything else.

In a busy world, our minds need rest. Use this book as a resource to help you tackle everyday pressure and emerge healthy and whole.

Each person deserves a day away in which no problems are confronted, no solutions searched for.

MAYA ANGELOU

CHAPTER ONE:

Calm Mornings

Step into your morning from a place of calm. Your day may be full of challenges, but you control the energy you bring to it. Five minutes spent centring yourself will benefit you and anyone who depends on you for the rest of the day.

Don't try to reinvent your morning. Instead, pick one or two tips from this chapter that will slip easily into your current routine, perhaps after your shower or before breakfast. Feel free to adapt these tips and create a morning routine that supports you all day long.

Picture your calm

Everything starts with an idea. Before we can create calm in our lives, we need to be able to imagine it. What does calm mean to you? How would you know if you are calmer today than you were yesterday? How would it affect your life? What would be happening today that wasn't happening yesterday? Before you get out of bed, spend a few moments thinking about what calm would look like for you today. Picture your day unfolding calmly. Once you see it, you'll believe it. Once you believe it, you'll create it.

LEARN TO CONNECT
WITH THE SILENCE
WITHIN. EVERYTHING
YOU WANT TO
MANIFEST IS WAITING
THERE TO SPROUT.

AMIT RAY

Survey your stressors

When thinking about your upcoming day, consider what might be the biggest source of stress. If you keep a daily journal, this could be a good time to write a few things down. Ask yourself: what is likely to be my biggest challenge today? And how do I want to face that challenge? You may not be able to change external forces, but you can change how you approach them. If you were to approach this potential stressor calmly, what would you do differently?

Make calm your mantra

A mantra is a positive saying we repeat to focus our thoughts. The great thing about a mantra is that you can say it while doing something else, such as when you're getting dressed or taking a shower — perfect for busy mornings. Find a calming mantra that works for you — maybe "I am calm" or "I choose to feel at peace" — or simply repeat the word "calm" a number of times.

Mindful morning

You might not have a lot of time to linger over breakfast or prepare for work or school in the morning, but whatever you do, do it mindfully. Mindfulness is all about being in the moment, free of distraction and focusing on the task at hand. This tip isn't asking for anything extra — instead, it's asking you to do what you usually would but with more focus. Focus creates stillness, and stillness becomes calm.

Write it down, work it out

If thoughts and worries whizz around your mind in the morning, decanting them onto a page is a great way to create distance and a sense of control. You can do this in a journal or diary; just let it all spill out onto a piece of paper. No one needs to read this but you. The process of writing will help to calm your mind and put your worries into perspective.

Gather strength, pull it in. Be right where you are.

JOY HARJO

Look up at the sky

You can complete this calming activity in under a minute, so aim to fit it in even during the busiest of times. Before starting your day, take a moment to engage with the bigger picture by looking to the sky above. What do you see? What's the weather like? Take a few deep breaths — how's the air this morning? Look up and survey the clouds: their shapes, color and movement. Even the greyest days will have shade and tone and differ from the day before. If you get up early enough, maybe you'll catch a sunrise with all its beautiful shifting colors. There's something very reassuring and calming about the fact that no matter what happened yesterday, the sun continues to rise, and so do we.

Follow the clouds with your eyes as they drift and travel. Can you see any birds up there? Count them and observe their path as they soar through the sky. By doing this, you're beginning to put your own challenges into perspective. The stresses of today will eventually move on, just like the birds and clouds above.

I closed my eyes to
look inward and found
a universe waiting
to be explored.

YUNG PUEBLO

Do a body scan

When you wake up in the morning, take a few moments to check in with your body and see how it's doing. Close your eyes and mentally direct your attention to each part of your body, working your way down from head to toe. Be grateful for everything that's feeling good and working well for you. And if you encounter any aches or pains, ask yourself calmly: what does my body need right now? By assessing yourself in this quiet way, you will grow in appreciation and awareness of who you are today.

Set an intention
to be calm today

We don't get to choose whether our day will be calm, but we do get to choose to meet any events calmly. So before your day gets going, set an intention to be calm.

An intention has power behind it. Think of the difference between hoping and intending to do something. The intention feels much more like the thing that's going to happen, doesn't it? It's an active step into creating the future you want to have.

Your intention is a totem to guide you through the day. It's a reminder of what you want to connect to. As you face choices and decisions, you can ask yourself: does this take me closer to or further away from my intention to be calm today? Sit with your intention and say it out loud — perhaps while you're looking in the bathroom mirror as you get ready for the day.

Five-minute yoga stretch

Many studies have found yoga to be an excellent stress reliever that promotes calmness and boosts well-being. There's never been an easier time to get your daily quick yoga fix, with free videos and guidance readily available via YouTube and Instagram, among other apps. Organize your morning stretch by preparing your space and some comfortable clothing the night before, and place them where you'll see them as soon as you wake up. In the morning, consider your needs. For example, if your day involves sitting at a desk, prepare by stretching your lower body.

With each sunrise,
we rise into
someone new.

ROXIE NAFOUSI

Sit still
and breathe

Breathe in. Hold it for a second or two. Now slowly breathe out. Feel calmer already? One of the best things we can do for our body and mind is to sit still and breathe. If you have a busy day coming up, deep breathing will help you focus and navigate it better. Sit somewhere secure and comfortable – perhaps on a chair or carpet. Close your eyes and breathe deeply in and out. Focusing only on your breath calms the nervous system and moves your mind from stress to relaxation. Reopen your eyes when it feels natural to do so.

Make breakfast
a ritual

Give yourself a little joy and pleasure by tweaking your morning routine and turning it into a more calming ritual. Save time by leaving out your favorite bowl or mug the night before. While you're at it, you could also prepare a nutritious breakfast in advance – perhaps some overnight oats, a fruit salad or some delicious granola. Take your food outside or look out of a window as you eat it and notice the wider world waking up.

Revisit your calm place

The answer to our search for calm is often already in our lives. Think about a time in the past when you felt particularly stressed. What helped you process that stress? What helped you return to a state of mindfulness? Was there a TV show you liked to watch, a hobby or activity you enjoyed, or a friend you spent time with? What has helped in the past that you're not doing now? Make a plan to incorporate this into your life again within the next week.

Next, think about the times when you felt most calm. What was going on then? Where were you? Who else was there? What made you feel calm? Recalling as many details as possible will help recreate how you felt and bring some of that calm from the past into the present. Thinking back to a calmer time is a way to give yourself a mental break from the pressures of today.

LEARN TO BE CALM
AND YOU WILL
ALWAYS BE HAPPY.

PARAMAHANSA YOGANANDA

Dress yourself calm

How we dress has a big impact on our feelings — think about the difference between wearing a business suit and loose loungewear. This has been called "dopamine dressing", which involves getting dressed with the intention of boosting your mood. What's your approach to getting dressed? Do you pull whatever's clean out of the wardrobe? Or whatever's least dirty off the floor? What would be a calmer way to dress and choose your clothing? According to color psychologists, greens and blues can be soothing and peaceful. Look at your wardrobe and choose clothing, textures and colors that you find calming.

Get grounded

Grounding, or "earthing" as it's sometimes known, is an ancient, calming practice where we physically connect to the natural world. This bond could be when you walk on grass with your bare feet or touch it with your hands. Research shows that physically connecting with the earth calms the nervous system, reduces inflammation and improves blood circulation, energy and general well-being.

Returning to nature can help you find a fresh perspective, particularly if you're not usually in the habit of walking outside barefoot. Before you put your shoes and socks on today, step outside for a moment and get grounded.

Almost everything
will work again if
you unplug it for
a few minutes,
including you.

ANNE LAMOTT

Progressive muscle relaxation

When we're anxious, our bodies often tense up without us noticing. Progressive relaxation can help release this tension. Start by sitting or lying down somewhere quiet where you won't be disturbed. You could even do this before getting out of bed in the morning.

Focus on one muscle group — your hands or feet, for instance. On an inhale, tense this area as hard as you can for 5 seconds. As you exhale, release the tension until that muscle group fully relaxes. Imagine your stress flowing out of your body. Repeat these steps for all the muscle groups in your body until you are completely at ease. Not only is this exercise relaxing, but it also helps you become aware of how both tension and calm feel in your body.

Self-care is the
non-negotiable.
That's the thing that
you have to do.

JONATHAN VAN NESS

Play with your pet

If you have a pet, they're probably keen for your attention in the morning, which is perfect for beginning your day with some love and calm. There's a reason why therapy animals are a thing – studies have shown that interacting with a pet for just a few minutes can significantly lower levels of the stress hormone, cortisol. Another study found that people who own pets have lower heart rates and blood pressure and can manage stressful situations more easily. For example, you could sit with your pet while practising deep breathing or spend time outside together barefoot.

Classical music

Listening to any kind of classical music has been found to lower blood pressure and help us feel calmer. Many scientific studies have linked listening to this type of music with reduced stress and anxiety. You don't need to have any specialist knowledge or understanding of the classics to absorb the benefits. Simply tune in to how you feel in response to the music.

Why not add a soundtrack to your morning with a classical radio station? Or perhaps listen to something if you commute to work. You could also make plans to go to a live concert sometime soon.

Five-minute meditation

Research has shown that just 5 minutes of meditation a day helps clear the mind, improve our mood, boost brain function, reduce stress and support a healthy metabolism. Another study found that people who meditate deal with negative feedback in a more impartial, less personalized way because of the improved levels of dopamine in their brains.

If you prefer guided meditation, during which a voice talks you through the session, you can find many 5-minute videos on YouTube and meditative podcasts to follow. You could even make a playlist of your favorites.

CHAPTER TWO:

Calm
Days

In this chapter, we'll look for ways to help us focus, stay on track and get more done, regardless of what else is happening. Your challenges and all the daily noise may remain, but you choose to approach them calmly. Your change might involve letting go of something stressful rather than adding more pressure to your already busy life.

Whether you spend your day at home, work or school, these ideas will help you sail through more smoothly. Pick out one or two tips and take them with you into your daily life.

Simplify your day

As the day starts, think about the upcoming 24 hours. Take out your diary if you keep one, and look at your schedule or timetable. What times are really crowded? How could you simplify that? Is there something that makes your heart sink? Did you sign up for a class or commitment that has turned out to take more than it gives? To avoid overwhelming yourself, decide to change or eliminate something cramping your day.

I will be calm.
I will be mistress
of myself.

JANE AUSTEN

Make your smartphone a calm zone

Our phones are one of the biggest culprits when it comes to interrupting our focus and inserting stress into our lives. But you own your phone; it doesn't own you, so you have a lot of choices when it comes to making sure it supports you rather than drains you. Making a few tweaks in how you use yours will have far-reaching benefits for your sense of calm.

Think about your current phone habits and what needs to change. Do at least one of these things today:

- Don't pick up your phone for the first hour of the day
- Turn off app notifications
- Swap scrolling through social media for a calming game
- Charge your phone outside of your bedroom
- Have a phone-free hour before bed
- Put your phone in another room when you're concentrating on a task

WE HEAR NOTHING
SO CLEARLY AS WHAT
COMES OUT OF SILENCE.

DAVID JAMES DUNCAN

Set your starting point

Think about your objectives today. What's the main thing you want to achieve? Break it down into the smallest actions, then identify where to start. That's your goal: not getting the whole thing done but finding an achievable, easy place to begin. Breaking it down like this will help you feel more in control and less overwhelmed. Don't think about completing the whole report. First, just open the document. Don't think about cleaning the whole house. Start by fetching the cleaning supplies. Find the easy place, the first step, and momentum will carry you calmly from there.

Counting for calm

Counting is an incredibly simple tool you can use any time you're finding stress to be overwhelming. Counting gives a whirring mind something to latch on to and, in the process, helps it slow and relax. Play with it to find out what suits you best. Some people find it much more calming to count backwards from ten to one than they do from one to ten. Others like to focus on counting something in particular — perhaps the number of cars you can see as you walk down the street or the shades of green growing in a garden.

That perfect
tranquillity of life,
which is nowhere
to be found but in
retreat, a faithful
friend and a
good library.

APHRA BEHN

Doodling

Studies have found that making art lowers levels of cortisol, regardless of whether it's aimless scribbling or something more advanced. Doodling has also been found to have mental health benefits, even when concentrating on something else, and you don't need any art skills at all to do it. If you're having trouble staying focused during a long online meeting, for example, a little absent-minded doodling could help you stay engaged.

Practise patience today

We live in a time of instant gratification. Anything we want can be delivered pretty much straight away, from food to entertainment. This means we need to practise being patient so we don't get overly stressed during those inevitable times when we have to wait for something. Try saving that TV show until the weekend or putting aside your favorite treat until the end of the work day. Walk out to a shop to buy something in person rather than ordering it online. Waiting calmly is a skill worth cultivating.

Create a
calming daily diet

Food has a huge impact on our mood, so plan your meals around how you want to feel. Magnesium is a particularly calming mineral found in many foods, including bananas, nuts and seeds, spinach and broccoli. Another food known to be both calming and incredibly nutritious is mango — and it makes a great snack!

As a restful accompaniment to your lunch today, why not seek out a calming tea? Many blends of herbal tea contain L-theanine, which can stimulate alpha waves in the brain, offering a sense of relaxation. Or you could stick to simple green tea, which has a small amount of caffeine for energy but also promotes calm and focus.

Reduce your consumption of food and drink known to potentially increase anxiety, such as caffeine, alcohol, processed foods, refined sugar and anything high in salt, as these are known to increase levels of cortisol. Keep it simple and natural — anything artificial is likely to put the body under strain and, therefore, create stress.

Remember
the quiet wonders.
The world has more
need of them than it
has for warriors.

CHARLES DE LINT

Challenge your mind calmly

Simple, repetitive puzzles have great calming powers since they put the brain into a meditative state. This is particularly beneficial if you are dealing with long-term stress. The aim here is to engage the brain in a way that's satisfying but not too complex. What sort of puzzles do you enjoy? A daily crossword, sudoku, dot-to-dot or jigsaw will give respite from the stress of the day and help you face your challenges more calmly.

Mindfulness walking

Walking has been found to be particularly effective in reducing symptoms of anxiety when combined with meditation. A great way to do this is via a mindfulness walk, where you aim to engage with your physical senses and stay in the moment. Take a short, mindful stroll today. Look up and around and consciously notice whatever your eyes land upon. Tune into your hearing and pick out the sounds all around you. Sniff the air to bring your sense of smell into play. Be in the moment and enjoy all its wonders.

There are some things
you learn best in calm,
and some in storm.

WILLA CATHER

Lunchtime yoga practice

While a morning yoga practice can be a great way to ease into the day calmly, inserting a little yoga into a busy lunchtime could be just what you need to get the energy to make it through to the evening. You can slip several yoga poses into your schedule, especially if you need to get out of your busy head and into your body.

The Bear Hug pose simply involves wrapping your arms around yourself and enjoying a deep back stretch. Then, because yoga is all about balance, swap your arms over so that the other one is on top and give yourself a second hug. This is a particularly good stretch to do after you've been hunched over a keyboard or stuck in a long online meeting. Yoga brings us back to breathing and slow, deliberate movements — a good reminder to be calm in a busy world.

BREATHING IN,
I CALM BODY AND
MIND. BREATHING OUT,
I SMILE. DWELLING IN
THE PRESENT MOMENT
I KNOW THIS IS THE
ONLY MOMENT.

THÍCH NHẠT HANH

Be the calm presence today

If you wish your daily environment was calmer, think about how that could start with you. How could you be the calm presence at work or college or wherever you spend your day? Being the steady rock will give you more authority and help other people feel calm and secure around you. We can't control how other people act and behave, but we can change how we act and behave, which will, in turn, influence everyone around us.

Bring nature indoors

Many studies have established the calming effects of being out in nature. It's also understood that just looking at photos of the natural world can reduce stress levels. So if your day is spent indoors under artificial light, bring nature to your workspace to enjoy the benefits. Have a screensaver that shows the loveliness of the great outdoors. Listen to the rhythmic sound of rain or wind. Put pictures of nature where you'll see them or bring back a souvenir, such as a stone or a leaf, from your next nature walk to keep on your desk.

Dive into blue

Color psychology has found that blue is the most calming color on the spectrum, so incorporate it into your daily life as much as possible. Lighter, softer blues tend to be the best for this, as they can also help us concentrate better. Look around your workspace — how much blue can you see? Try looking out at the sky from time to time, wearing blue, painting your nails or putting images of water where you will see them regularly.

Create a
calm space

Create a calm corner and use it to recharge every day. Carve out an undisturbed, clutter-free space wherever you spend most of your time — it can be as small as a desk drawer or even a pinboard. Moving to another part of the room where you have an alternative view can also be restful. How about your commute? Is there potential for calm there? Or could you perhaps take your lunch in a different environment, like a park or café?

I use breath to
connect me to the
present moment
and to create space
in my body.

TRACEE ELLIS ROSS

Digital declutter

Ridding ourselves of excess physical clutter can help us feel freer. The same is true for digital clutter. Take a look at your main computer screen — what's on there that doesn't need to be? How many tabs do you usually have open? And how many need to be there? Keeping them open means at least a small part of your mind isn't on the task at hand. If available, consider using browsers or programs in "full screen" mode to avoid distraction.

Then look at the digital clutter on your phone. Which of those apps have you not used in the last six months and are unlikely to use again? Deleting them takes seconds, so give it a go! Group any apps you only use occasionally into a single folder. That way, they're still there when you need them, but the home screen is less busy.

Think about how you could deal with emails more calmly, perhaps by only going through them at certain times of the day rather than letting them interrupt your focus as and when they come in.

Follow the birds

Listening to birdsong, even in recorded form, has been found to improve well-being and help us feel less stressed. Birds in flight can also be incredibly calming to watch — think of the elegant, hypnotic mass of a starling murmuration. To encourage birds into your daily space, you could put up a small bird feeder outside of a window where you can see it regularly or take a quick trip to a local park.

Choose to find calmness
within yourself, and make
it your superpower.

ANGEL CHERNOFF

CHAPTER THREE:

Calm
Evenings

If you've had a hectic day, the evening can come as a sigh of relief. The evening is your time to wind down and process the day just gone, then prepare for the next one. You decide how calm you want your evening to be.

Later in the day can be lively, but it can also be a time to recharge both physically and mentally. The tools and tips in this chapter will help you create an evening that supports you rather than drains you. For tomorrow to be calmer, the path towards that destination starts tonight.

Take an evening tech break

If you've been using technology throughout the day, the evening is the time to give your brain a break from it. When spending time with friends and family, be 100 per cent present with them by leaving your phone or laptop in another room.

The blue light from most screens disrupts our biological clock and isn't recommended for a good night's sleep. The less you see it this evening, the more your sleep will benefit. Give your phone an earlier bedtime than yours and tuck it up snugly somewhere out of sight until morning. You'll both sleep more soundly as a result!

Everybody should just stay
at home and meditate and
they'd be so much happier.

GEORGE HARRISON

I CLOSE MY EYES
AND LISTEN TO THE
VOICES OF THE RAIN.

ROBIN WALL KIMMERER

Foot massage

If you've been on your feet all day, take the opportunity to rest for a few minutes and look after the limbs that supported you. For a little acupressure massage and stress relief combined, you could roll a tennis ball or something similar under the arches of each foot. This is particularly important if you expect to be on your feet again tomorrow — think of this pause as a time to look after your most precious tool, your body.

Leave work at work

If you work or study from home, it can easily feel like you're never off the clock. But it's essential to have some wind-down time to process whatever you've just done and prepare your body and mind for sleep. You'll face the challenges of tomorrow better if you've had some time off tonight.

Decide on a time at which you will stop working and stick to it. Put away the computer and any paperwork. Close the door on your workspace if you can. Avoid checking emails once the working day is over. And plan to do something fun and non-work-related afterwards. Perhaps enjoy a good meal, talk to a friend or watch something you love on TV. When you're working hard and have a deadline to meet, this break is essential. Remember that taking a few minutes to relax will help you work better tomorrow.

Connect calmly to your intuition

As nighttime is usually quieter, this is an ideal opportunity to listen to your intuition, the quiet voice of wisdom inside us all. Intuitive thoughts focus on the present and tend to feel quite neutral or calm. Start by using it in small ways — what's your gut instinct telling you to eat for dinner or do with your evening? Learning to listen to your intuition will enable you to meet stressful situations with a calm approach and logic that speaks to you personally.

The
ordinary acts
we practise every
day at home are of
more importance to
the soul than their
simplicity might
suggest.

THOMAS MOORE

Calming candles

What is it about a flickering candle flame that's so calming and relaxing? The low light has been found to induce a meditative state, as our brains associate it with relaxation. Light a candle in the evening to create a relaxing ambience, or try a form of meditation called Trataka, also known as "candle gazing". This method involves looking at a fixed point (the flame) and using it as a focus for meditation.

Relax
your jaw

Tightness in the jaw muscles is very common, as this is one part of the body where stress and anxiety can often settle. If your jaw is achy after a difficult day, focus on relaxing it via massage or gently rotating the mandible (lower jaw) around, breathing deeply as you go. Moving your jaw around will help the blood to flow and relieve any aches that have gathered there.

A calm evening meal

What we eat in the evening affects our quality of sleep, so keep your evening meal light, nourishing and easily digestible. Choose natural, unprocessed foods as much as possible. Be sure to include some protein for longer-lasting energy to get you through until breakfast. Eat your meal away from screens and with your phone in another room. Practising mindfulness while you eat will help build your focus in other areas of life.

Fruit and vegetables will give you the nutrients to help you feel calmer. Vitamin B (found in cucumber, broccoli and leafy greens) helps relax the nervous system. Potassium and magnesium promote a good mood and can be found in carrots, kiwi fruit, bananas, pears and plums. Many fruits and vegetables are also high in vitamin C, which helps reduce stress and is great for your immune system.

When we focus on trying to fix the problem, it is easy to underestimate the power of simply being there.

DR JULIE SMITH

Gratitude

At the end of the day, practising gratitude is a powerful way to reconnect to the good things in your life. What three things are you grateful for right now? Even if the day was challenging, be grateful that you made it through. As you seek out the positive things and people in your life, you will naturally start to notice more of them. This will also help you build resilience so that when bad things do happen, you can see them in perspective as part of a whole that is largely good.

Give yourself a worry window

If there's something bothering you, these worries can creep into your life at any time and make you feel stressed. Instead, take active charge of your concerns and allow yourself a 5-minute worry window in the evening. This is your time to focus on the things that bug you. Having an active beginning and end to your worry window will help you control when your worries are on your mind, build an awareness of how you experience them and, most importantly, train you to disengage with them when you're ready.

In the madness,
you have to
find calm.

LUPITA NYONG'O

ASMR

Autonomous sensory meridian response, or ASMR, refers to the experience of a pleasurable tingling sensation triggered by particular stimuli, such as gentle movement and quiet sounds. The areas of the brain activated by ASMR are associated with hormones like dopamine, oxytocin and endorphins, all of which can promote feelings of calm and relaxation. Not everyone responds to ASMR – National Geographic found that around 10–20 per cent of us are "tingleheads" – but it's easily accessible.

Check out some of the many online ASMR videos featuring creators who speak quietly and use a range of materials to make gentle, soothing sounds. There's little official research to prove that ASMR helps you sleep better, but anecdotally many people say they find it very effective in helping them get to sleep. One study noted that 80 per cent of people who used ASMR said it positively affected their mood, and the benefits lasted for many hours.

Snuggle under a weighted blanket

A weighted blanket can help you feel more relaxed and may be a good comforter to aid a good night's sleep. Studies have found that these blankets may prove particularly helpful in relieving anxiety. Weighted blankets, as the name suggests, are typically much heavier than the usual woollen blanket. They're also known as therapy blankets since they simulate deep pressure therapy (DPT). This provides a similar comforting physiological response to the sensation we get when we're being held or hugged.

Become calmer by crying

If you start to feel emotional in the evening, perhaps when watching a TV show, and feel tears welling up, don't hold back. Crying releases stress and emotional pain. You'll feel calmer after crying for very simple biological reasons. Researchers have established that crying releases oxytocin and endogenous opioids, also known as endorphins. These feel-good chemicals help ease both physical and emotional pain. Tears are a stress reliever, with studies finding that over 50 per cent of people reported an improved mood after crying.

DO NOT APOLOGIZE
FOR CRYING. WITHOUT
THIS EMOTION, WE
ARE ONLY ROBOTS.

ELIZABETH GILBERT

Pause to find the learning from today

You may have had a stressful day today, but that doesn't mean you have to carry those stresses into tomorrow. Take time to ask yourself, or perhaps write in a journal or notebook, what you learned today that you can use tomorrow. What can you take from today that's good? By focusing on the lessons you can take from today, you're positively using your challenges, which will help you feel more in control. You're not a victim of what happens to you. You're a survivor who lives to thrive another day.

Have a
sleep routine

A good night's sleep is something to slide calmly into. An overburdened mind will likely disturb you all night long, so create a pre-sleep routine to relax your mind and help you rest. Having regular bedtime habits also signals to your mind that it's time to go to sleep and makes it easier for you to do so in the future.

What do you enjoy enough to want to do every evening as part of your bedtime routine? Perhaps some yoga stretches, reading a few pages of a book or a meditation exercise? If a shower or a hot bath helps you relax, add them into your nighttime schedule. Keep to the same bedtime and wake time every day, even at the weekend, as much as possible. Your brain will get used to this pattern and be more likely to respond to the rhythm.

A cup of camomile

Make it a priority to avoid caffeine in the evening, as it may disturb your sleep. As much as possible, sidestep caffeine after 3 p.m. Instead, opt for decaffeinated and herbal teas if you want a hot drink later in the day. Camomile tea has long been used as a traditional remedy for a wide range of afflictions, from hay fever to insomnia, and scientists have investigated how it might help with various ailments. Several studies have noted its effectiveness in helping people sleep, so make it part of your calming evening routine.

You are the sky.
Everything else – it's
just the weather.

PEMA CHÖDRÖN

Set an intention for tomorrow

Just as we started this morning by setting an intention for the day, it's a good idea to round off your evening by setting an intention for tomorrow. Look at your schedule or timetable and see what's coming up in the next 24 hours. You might want to write a to-do list from the calm of tonight before you jump into the thick of it tomorrow. Ask yourself: what one word will be your calm guiding light for tomorrow? How do you intend to be tomorrow? Remember, your intention is less an objective and more a totem to direct you.

CHAPTER FOUR:

Calm
Ever After

So far we've looked at tips that will slot easily into your day. But since we're aiming to embrace a sustainable calmer life, let's look at how to do it in the longer term. Just as stress is always present in life, we will always need some peace and quiet to counteract it.

This chapter contains tips that will allow you to enjoy an oasis of calm in the future. Think of them as seeds you plant, growing into a calmer tomorrow. In giving this gift to Future You, you're taking care of yourself today.

Seek out a quiet space

Sometimes the simplest way to find calm is to go to places already quiet and peaceful by nature — perhaps a library or an art gallery. You don't need any special knowledge to enjoy the exhibitions and displays. Just sit quietly in the space, look at what's in front of you and consider how it makes you feel. Check out what's available locally that sounds interesting to you, and make a plan to go there this week.

Make like Taylor Swift and shake it off

Physical movement is one of the best things for dealing with stress and becoming calmer. The rhythmic nature of moving your body and raising your heart rate a little will help to get you out of your head and away from your cares and worries. You'll also increase your endorphins and feel happier as a result.

But formal exercise classes aren't for everybody, so the challenge here is simply to pause and think of a way to move your body that you enjoy. You could add a dance break into your day and shake your cares away to your favorite tunes. Or go outside and walk, run or skip in the fresh air. Make a date to go swimming, hiking, hula-hooping or trampolining at the weekend. Find a yoga video you love. Decide now how you're going to shake it off today and tomorrow.

Know that there is
a time coming in your life
when dirt settles and the
patterns form a picture.

YRSA DALEY-WARD

Create a calming playlist

Music is an incredibly powerful way to shift our mood, so how about creating a playlist that will help you relax and feel calmer? Our response to music is unique to our own life experience, so your calming playlist doesn't necessarily have to contain only gentle tunes. It could be loud rock if that's what you love and enjoy listening to. Often the music that puts us in our comfort zone is the stuff we're most connected to, so maybe add some songs that you associate with happy and relaxed times in your life.

Have fun
with fidget toys

Fidget toys can be a great way to channel excess physical energy and calm you down in stressful situations. They can be particularly useful during online meetings where your hands aren't on show. You can use them off-camera to appear calmer and more confident on screen, like a swan gliding smoothly as they kick underwater.

Many gadgets like this are available, or you might prefer a squashy toy or some bubble wrap. Or use something that's already available — if you wear a ring, it can be comforting to stroke or spin around on your finger.

The quieter you
become, the more
you can hear.

RAM DASS

Get creative

What creative project do you feel drawn to? What do you see yourself having completed in the future? It could be writing a novel, creating art, undertaking a music project or building a business. Or even a small creative activity such as cross-stitch, knitting or drawing. When you look at the project as a whole, it might seem overwhelming, but breaking it down will make it more manageable. And this process of planning can be quite calming as you start to get a handle on things and become more in control of your life rather than drifting and feeling dissatisfied.

Breaking a project down into small chunks means it's much more doable. And over time, all of those chunks will add up. The time will pass anyway, so why not use it to create something you've always wanted to? Not only will you gain a new skill and something fun or beautiful to show for it, but the patience and process required can also be applied to many other elements of daily life.

Create a calm workspace

Look around your workspace and ask yourself honestly: does this seem like a place of calm or chaos? How many unfinished projects and unnecessary things are around you right now? Tidying and clearing the desktop clutter will help your mind become calmer and more focused. What is in your workspace right now that doesn't need to be there? Remove it and add a plant or something you picked up on a nature walk. A calming workspace will promote clarity of thought and allow you to work without distraction.

Retreat quietly

What would you do with some time just to yourself? Artists and religious orders have long used retreats to seek some respite from the turbulence of the world, but anyone can benefit from pausing to reset. Plan out a retreat for yourself. It doesn't need to be somewhere isolated — just away from your usual daily life, and probably solo. If you bring a phone with you, keep it silent and in a bag and go off-grid for an hour, a day or as long as you choose. Just think of it as a date with yourself.

First-aid calm kit

When we get stressed, it's easy to lose perspective and forget about the things that can restore our calm. So take time to gather together your emergency calm accessories. Include anything that restores your spirits — perhaps your favorite caffeine-free tea blend, a wise book you love, a puzzle or a relaxing scented candle. Think of it like a first-aid kit for your mind — better to have one and not need it than to need one and not have it. Gather the materials together and put them somewhere easily accessible, like a bag or backpack.

EVERY DAY
I CREATE SPACE FOR
MY SOUL TO BREATHE.

NTATHU ALLEN

Set peace of mind
as your highest goal,
and organize your
life around it.

BRIAN TRACY

Be by water

There's a lot of scientific evidence stating that water makes us feel calm – even to the point where simply drinking a glass of water can calm our nerves. Studies have shown that people who live by water are calmer than those in more landlocked environments. This phenomenon is known as "blue health" – so make a plan to get to the water soon. Perhaps you could visit the beach, walk along the river, take part in some outdoor swimming or even have a long bath. Put a water bottle in your workspace as a reminder to keep hydrated every day.

Find connection

Sometimes when we can't see the wood for the trees, it takes another person to lead us out of the forest. Talking to a friend can be all it takes to help you put things in perspective, but it has to be the right kind of person. A friend that's all about the drama maybe isn't the right person for a stressful day. Who do you know that is particularly empathetic, has a calming presence and that you always feel good after talking to? Make it a priority to spend time with them soon.

If you can't find this person in your life, think of people you admire as being particularly calm and seek out their content — perhaps books, podcasts or videos. And if you've been working on some of the suggestions in this book, perhaps you could be someone else's calm point in a storm. Make a calm connection today.

More magnesium

We've mentioned adding the mineral magnesium to your daily diet, but you can also take a supplement for more ongoing benefits. Magnesium has been the subject of many studies in recent years, with research showing that it helps the brain deal with stress and anxiety by restricting the release of stress hormones such as cortisol. This has seen it dubbed "nature's tranquillizer". Add magnesium-rich foods, such as dark chocolate, avocado, nuts, seeds, bananas and tofu, to your daily meals. Remember to consult your doctor or physician before adjusting your diet with supplements.

Close your eyes.
Hear the silent snow.
Listen to your soul speak.

ADRIENNE POSEY

You can't calm the storm,
so stop trying. What you
can do is calm yourself.
The storm will pass.

TIMBER HAWKEYE

Forgiveness

Unfinished business can be one of the most unsettling aspects of life because it's still broken and incomplete. This is as true for unfinished household projects as it is for unfinished emotional business. What has happened in your past that is still bugging you today? Make a plan to move on, fuelled by forgiveness. Who has done you wrong in the past that you need to forgive today? Is there anything you need to forgive yourself for? Write a letter stating: "I forgive you for..." and then throw it away as a symbolic act of letting go.

A calming scent

Scent is another powerful way to change how we feel, so use it to your advantage. Lavender is known to be particularly calming, so if you have space to plant some lavender, you could enjoy its calming benefits for years to come. Scientists have also found that the scent of a romantic partner can be relaxing – this is why snuggling up to your loved one's old T-shirt is so enjoyable. Other relaxing scents include camomile, rose, bergamot and jasmine. Incorporate these in your life via oil diffusers, scented candles, body lotion or bath oil.

Plan a trip

Psychologists have found that having something to look forward to can lift our mood. It puts today's worries into a separate context by showing us that something better is on its way. Take a few moments to plan a future trip — anything from somewhere new in your neighborhood you want to explore to a full-blown dream holiday. Put a date in a diary or calendar for when you plan to go.

It's OK to say "no"

A lack of calm can be a sign that you are overwhelmed. With a lot going on already, think very carefully about whatever else you take into your life. Don't say yes in the moment if you think you may regret it later. Be proud of when you say no and stick to your boundaries. An overwhelmed life will never be calm and is most likely heading for burnout.

It's OK to calmly push back when too much is being asked of you today. If you need to say no, don't over-explain or rush to apologize — a simple but polite "Thank you for thinking of me, but I won't be able to do that" is enough. Adopt a personal policy of never agreeing to anything in the moment. Saying "Let me get back to you" gives you time to pause and consider whether this really is a good thing for you to do right now — or would your life be calmer without adding more commitments to your plate?

Conclusion

Creating a daily calm space for yourself is an essential part of self-care. You have to take care of yourself in order to help those who might depend on you. In this fast-moving world, know that you deserve some peace and calm, and as we've discovered, it is easy to find when you know where to look.

It only takes 5 minutes to connect to calm, but the benefits will support you through the day. As we've seen throughout this book, being calm carries immense physical and mental health benefits. Which tips resonated with you most and what will you do to choose calm today?

Be the still water. Detach from the noise to find calm. Look within yourself to a quiet centre and feel refreshed.

Have you enjoyed this book?
If so, find us on Facebook at
Summersdale Publishers,
on Twitter at @Summersdale
and on Instagram and TikTok
at @summersdalebooks and get in
touch. We'd love to hear from you!

www.summersdale.com